The Artful Cookie

The Artful Cookie

Baking & Decorating
Delectable Confections

Aaron Morgan

LARK BOOKS

A Division of Sterling Publishing Co., Inc.
New York

The Library of Congress has cataloged the hardcover edition as follows:

Morgan, Aaron.
   The artful cookie : baking & decorating delectable confections / Aaron
Morgan.
      p. cm.
Includes index.
   ISBN 1-57990-484-X
   1. Cookies. 2. Cake decorating. I. Title.
TX772.M67 2004
641.8'654--dc22

                                                              2003017070

Editor:
Valerie Van Arsdale Shrader

Art Director:
Tom Metcalf

Photographer:
Sandra Stambaugh

Cover Designer:
Barbara Zaretsky

Associate Art Director:
Shannon Yokeley

Editorial Assistance:
Delores Gosnell

10 9 8 7 6 5 4 3 2 1

Published by Lark Books, a division of
Sterling Publishing Co., Inc.
387 Park Avenue South, New York, N.Y. 10016

First Paperback Edition 2006
© 2004, Aaron Morgan

Distributed in Canada by Sterling Publishing,
c/o Canadian Manda Group, 165 Dufferin Street
Toronto, Ontario, Canada M6K 3H6

Distributed in the United Kingdom by GMC Distribution Services,
Castle Place, 166 High Street, Lewes, East Sussex, England BN7 1XU

Distributed in Australia by Capricorn Link (Australia) Pty Ltd.,
P.O. Box 704, Windsor, NSW 2756 Australia

If you have questions or comments about this book, please contact:
Lark Books
67 Broadway
Asheville, NC 28801
(828) 253-0467

Manufactured in China

ISBN 13: 978-1-57990-484-5 (hardcover) 978-1-57990-955-0 (paperback)
ISBN 10: 1-57990-484-X (hardcover) 1-57990-955-8 (paperback)

For information about custom editions, special sales, premium and corporate purchases, please contact Sterling Special Sales Department at 800-805-5489 or specialsales@sterlingpub.com.

Table of Contents

Introduction

What is an artful cookie? It's a cookie that's not only stunning to behold but absolutely delicious, a delight for all the senses. It's a luscious dollop of ganache perched atop a base of short-bread, dipped in white chocolate and covered with streams of colored glaze. It's also a simple snowflake, sparkling like a diamond from the coarse sugar scattered over its surface. You'll find dozens of them on the pages that follow.

As a professional pastry chef, it's my job to be well versed in all aspects of baking, from breads to classic desserts and cakes. Throughout my career, how-ever, one discipline of baking has always had a special place in my heart: cookies. My earliest memory of

baking is having my mother put me to work cutting and decorating cookies for the holidays. Mom provided me with the dough, baker's board, rolling pin, cutters, sheet pans, and decorat-ing materials. Then I was on my own, creating cookies! Well, Mom, would you have imagined? Those early sessions in the kitchen led to 20 years of crafting recipes and creating desserts for a living.

It's no wonder it all started with cook-ies. At its heart, a cookie is basic, and making a good cookie requires little time and few ingredients, which is what makes baking cookies a great activity for children of all ages. You'll find the recipes in this book easy to mix and my

decorating methods fairly simple. My favorite thing to do, in fact, is to take something basic and easily turn it into something more—sometimes sophisti-cated, sometimes stylish, sometimes playful—but always delectable in addi-tion to being beautiful. I use chocolate glazes as my primary decorating medi-um, because they're easy to prepare and produce cookies that simply taste extraordinary. Who can resist a breath-taking, buttery cookie drenched in chocolate? To embellish them, I'll show you how to use a parchment paper cone to create Belgian lace and elegant loops called draping. You'll also learn to grace your cookies with colored sug-ars, dragées (those pretty, edible metal-

lic balls), candies, royal icing, and its more vivid variation, color flow.

But an artful cookie doesn't have to be a decorated one. Many of the designs I've included are attractive in their construction alone and may have only the most minimal embellishment—a sprinkle of powdered sugar, perhaps, or a drizzle of chocolate. The crimped apricot pockets on page 80 are elegantly crafted cookies, for example, and the swank two-toned twists on page 32 are merely braided cookie dough. Each of these is a delightful example of how you can create a lovely confection without elaborate decoration.

In the following pages, I'll teach you how to take the basic cookie and trans-

form it into the divine, taking you step by step through the process of making your own creative cookies. Most of the designs can be made with any of the four basic dough recipes provided, and four easy recipes for glaze, ganache, and royal icing add the decorative touches. Once you master the professional secrets I share and develop a feel for the basic techniques I use, I hope you'll set your imagination free to design, twist, crimp, color, and adorn your own deliciously artful cookies.

lumps in the sugar and bring the butter to a consistent texture so it's evenly distributed in the dough. It's not necessary to cream butter and sugar for a long time. Once they're blended together, it's time to add any liquids, like eggs or flavor extracts.

Flour is usually the last ingredient added. Then, mix *just enough* to combine all the ingredients. This is the critical point in making a great-tasting, melt-in-your-mouth cookie. Too much mixing will develop gluten, which is a protein in the flour that gives dough elasticity. While the presence of gluten is desirable in bread making, it's unwanted in cookie baking, because the dough will be tough and more difficult to manipulate, and the finished cookie will not have the proper texture or taste. When you're mixing the dough, don't forget to scrape the bottom of the bowl with a rubber spatula to incorporate all the ingredients.

The majority of the projects in this book are rolled cookies. To make them, you must refrigerate the fresh dough for at least 4 hours after preparing it. Don't work all the dough at once; take just a batch at a time and leave the rest to stay cool in the refrigerator. Knead it by hand to get a smooth consistency. Even though the dough needs to stay cool, you're warming the butter as you work, which makes the dough soft. The cooler your dough is as you work it, the better your results will be. Keep the dough refrigerated as much as possible.

Baking the Artful Cookie

A stylish cookie doesn't require many specialized tools or equipment, just creativity and resourcefulness. If you've made a chocolate chip cookie or decorated a cake, you probably have the basic equipment you'll need in your kitchen. The ingredients, too, are basic—flour, butter, sugar, eggs, extracts…and of course chocolate. Before you get artistic with the cookie, you must first make the proper dough.

Here are the key points in making and manipulating cookie dough; a discussion of recommended tools follows. The recipes themselves begin on page 20, and the cookie designs start on page 25.

Preparing the Dough

Start with soft butter. With an electric mixer, cream the butter and sugar at medium speed until the mixture becomes a smooth paste; break up any

Keep even pressure as you roll; this produces a dough of uniform thickness.

Be sure to use enough flour to keep the dough from sticking to your work surface or the rolling pin. When you use a rolling pin, it's important to keep even pressure on the surface of the dough. There's a tendency to apply too much pressure to the center of the dough and not enough on the edges, resulting in an uneven thickness in the finished cookies. They'll bake inconsistently and won't look the same if this occurs. Roll the dough from one end to the other, edge to edge, with even pressure. Make sure the dough is not sticking to any surface so it can expand while you're rolling.

Flour any knives and cutters by dipping them in flour and tapping off the excess. After your cookies are cut, brush off any excess flour with a pastry brush. Then, work the remaining dough in batches as described above.

Some of the designs require fusing pieces of dough. For this procedure, use a little water or beaten egg and then press the parts together. The pieces will then fuse and not separate while they're being baked.

Using Margarine

Margarine can be used in place of butter in these recipes. Margarine has a higher melting point, which means more stability in working with the dough, and it costs less than butter. But, butter gives cookies the best flavor. My rule is to use margarine when the cookies are purely decorative. But since you also want to be able to savor the beautiful cookies presented here, I suggest you use butter. It's more than worth a little more trouble in the process, and there's simply no substitute for its flavor.

Baking the Cookies

350°F is a safe temperature for most cookies. The types of dough used in *The Artful Cookie* will bake with very little color; slight browning on the edges is plenty. If they bake any darker, the cookies will become very brittle. They will be fragile when cool and more difficult to decorate. I must stress, however, that each oven is different, and the baking times given here are guidelines only. Always start with the shortest time suggested, and be sure to use a timer—it takes only a few minutes for a perfectly baked cookie to become overbaked. And, as you probably know, you should always preheat the oven before baking.

Decorating the Artful Cookie

I use chocolate glazes to decorate the majority of the cookies in this book. I think they look and taste better than cookies created with royal icing. Because royal icing and its variation, color flow, are made with raw egg whites, they make some people nervous, but when the egg whites dry the cookies are perfectly safe. Royal icing and color flow do have a place in cookie decorating, as you'll see in designs like the flat gingerbread house and the flower basket, and you can use pasteurized egg whites if you so desire.

Decorating with Chocolate Glazes

Chocolate glazes are ready to use as soon as they're melted, and they must remain in a liquid state while you're working. White and semisweet dark chocolate bars are available in most stores, though milk chocolate can also be used. Bars are better than chips, because the chips tend to be too thick when melted and may need a drop or two of vegetable oil to thin. Chips are an economical alternative, however.

To prepare the glaze, chop about 1½ or 2 cups of chocolate and place it in a microwave-safe bowl. Microwave first for a minute; stir the chocolate and microwave again for 45 seconds to 1 minute. The chocolate must melt gently, because it burns very easily. Chocolate can surprise you, because it will hold its shape in the microwave even if it's melting. Keep stirring and returning the chocolate to the microwave until it's melted smooth. The more liquid chocolate you have in your bowl, though, the less time it will need in the microwave. If the chocolate sets while you're working, repeat this process to melt it again. The tried-and-true double-boiler technique—*Bain Marie* in culinary terms—can also be used to melt chocolate, of course.

Although you can microwave chocolate on high power, you must be attentive to it and stir well between cooking sessions; chocolate is delicate. If you can reduce the power while you're melting the chocolate, so much the better. Unlike dark chocolate, white chocolate has no cocoa mass and will thus burn more quickly; it needs to be monitored carefully while preparing a glaze.

It's *imperative* to use only powdered or oil-based food colors when making a colored chocolate glaze. Most liquid colors are water based, as are many pastes and gels. Water is chocolate's enemy, as even a single drop will alter the consistency of the chocolate, making it thicker, and the effects cannot be reversed. To color white chocolate, divide the melted chocolate into small bowls as needed, but wait until you're ready to work with each color before preparing it. It's easier to keep one large bowl of chocolate melted than to keep a rainbow of colors melted. Add the coloring a little at a time, because it's easy to use too much. You can always add more if you're not satisfied with the shade.

Chocolates look best and blend best for designs and marbling when they're still melted, so work quickly. When you're using several colors at a time, as in many of the designs in this book, you can keep them in a melted state by placing the chocolates in a warm oven, on as low a temperature as possible. Check them frequently to be sure the chocolates don't overheat, and rotate

them in and out of the oven if they get too warm. An alternative method is to place the bowls of glaze in a larger bowl or pan of warm water.

There are several ways to apply the chocolate glazes. Many of the cookies are first dipped in the glaze, while others have details that are created with a parchment paper cone filled with the glaze. (Chocolate glaze is too liquid to allow the use of a pastry bag and decorating tips.) See page 18 to learn how to make your own parchment cone. The individual designs will illustrate the techniques I used, but see the photos on page 19 for a demonstration of the types of embellishment you can achieve with a piping cone. If you're creating texture, like raised piping or borders, allow the dipped cookies to set before adding details. If you haven't done much decorating, practice the tech-

niques before you begin creating cookies in earnest.

Decorating with Royal Icing and Color Flow

Royal icing is a staple of cake and cookie decorating. It's excellent for decorative piping, flowers, and borders because it sets and holds its shape. Color flow is a modification of royal icing, where you add color to the white royal icing and thin it into a thick liquid with additional egg white. It's a little simpler to use color flow than colored chocolates, frankly, because you can use any type of food coloring (powder, gel, etc.), and the color flow doesn't have to stay warm like the colored glazes. But I still prefer the taste and appearance of chocolate and think the extra effort is justified.

You'll find the recipe for royal icing on page 24. To make color flow, first add the color and then thin the icing with additional egg white. Be sure to add the color first, because some colorings, especially the liquid ones, may alter the consistency of the icing. Because both royal icing and color flow will begin to form a crust in a matter of minutes, you must keep either one moist and covered tightly with a damp towel when not in use. Stir the icing frequently while you're decorating. Color flow will harden completely in a matter of hours, royal icing a little more quickly. This hardening process dries out and cures the egg whites, producing a similar result to that obtained from a standard food dehydrating procedure.

Apply royal icing with a pastry bag and tips. If you want to use the same icing for more than one effect, get a coupler for your pastry bag that allows you to use multiple tips with the same bag. Read a little more about using a pastry bag on page 17. If you're piping with color flow, you'll need to use a parchment cone.

Decorating with Colored Sugar or Coconut

You can also create beautiful effects with colored sugars, as you'll see in the frosted flowers on page 48. (They are also shown below.) Use powdered food color for this technique, because it doesn't add moisture to the granulated sugar. Liquid colors can also work, but may cause some lumping in the granules. To color sugar, simply place it in a container, add color, and shake to blend. (Reclosable plastic bags are great for this process.) The colored sugars can be sprinkled on cookies, but for more precise application, brush the area of the cookie to be colored with water and dip it into the sugar. You can also color coconut in the same manner, although liquid colors work well, too

Decorating with Candy

To see what a mesmerizing effect melted candy can add to a cookie, look at the butterscotch stars on page 26. To incorporate candy into a design, crush the hard candies with a hammer (food processors can work with a small amount of candy). Cut out a cavity in the cookies and bake them until they're about three-quarters done. Place the crushed hard candies into the cookies and return them to the oven until the candy melts clear. Don't allow the candy to boil, as this will ruin the smooth appearance.

The Artful Implements

Here is a list of the basic tools and equipment you should have on hand to create stylish cookies. Turn the page to read a bit about the use of these items.

measuring cups and spoons

kitchen mixer

metal bowls

wooden spoons

heavy-duty saucepan

rolling pin

baker's board (breadboard)

cookie cutters

cutter sets

pizza cutter (dough wheel)

paring knife and chef's knife
  (French knife)

cookie stamps

spatulas (pallet knives), especially a
  small offset spatula

sculpting tools

mini muffin pan

baking sheets

silicone baking mat

cooling rack

parchment paper and aluminum foil

pastry bags and/or disposable
  pastry bags

couplers and pastry tips

pastry brush

paintbrushes

ruler and/or clear acrylic strip

scissors

Here are brief descriptions of the tools and equipment you need to create memorable cookies. Use the list of basic implements on the preceding page as you gather your supplies; any additional or specialty items are listed in the project instructions.

To begin, be sure to use your *measuring cups and spoons*. Baking is a science! Save a "pinch of this" and a "touch of that" for your soup, and rely on strict measurements to create distinctive cookies.

If you have a heavy-duty *kitchen mixer*, use the flat paddle attachment to mix the dough, which will make easy work of any recipe. A handheld mixer will work, too, and if no other options present themselves, the reliable metal bowl and heavy wooden spoon will suffice. Again, soft butter will make your job infinitely easier.

You need a *rolling pin* and a flat surface with lots of work space to process the dough. Remember to use plenty of flour so your dough doesn't stick to the surface or the rolling pin. A *baker's board*, or breadboard, can help keep your kitchen clean; place it on your counter as your work surface. A *pastry brush* will help you clean off any excess flour from the dough.

There are many options for cutting dough. *Cookie cutters* of all shapes and sizes are a must to produce confections like the ones in *The Artful Cookie*. Sets of cutters allow you to choose

from a progression of sizes. *Templates*, which you can make yourself, are great for custom designs. A *pizza cutter*, also known as a dough wheel, is great for long, straight cuts because the rolling blade doesn't stretch or drag the dough, which maintains the intended shape of the cookie. *Paring knives* are great for detailed cuts and corners. A *chef's knife*, also called a French knife, is great for chopping ingredients and cutting cookie dough in designs such as the macaroon on page 82 or the checkerboard on page 44.

Stamps and *sculpting tools* add engaging details, edges, or patterns to the unbaked cookie. Other found tools can add inventive touches; a *toothpick* can make a nice "stitching" pattern, for instance, and a *pasta wheel* can make interesting edges while cutting dough. Be creative, because anything with a raised texture can conceivably work to emboss a cookie; an inexpensive sun catcher was used on the design on page 88.

Rulers or clear acrylic strips are great for cutting strips, squares, and rectangles, as well as making measured cuts and straight lines.

Spatulas, also called pallet knives, are marvelous for handling cookies without damaging decorations or leaving telltale finger indentations. A small offset spatula is perfect for really delicate handling, as its design allows you to easily get underneath the cookies. This tool is also a good choice for spreading icing

or chocolate onto small surfaces. Larger spatulas are of course appropriate for handling several cookies at a time if you're baking a quantity of goods.

Obviously, you'll need *baking sheets*, but you also may want to invest in a *silicone baking mat*, because it can be used for all types of baking. The silicone prevents sticking, so these mats are perfect for delicate work such as the fortune cookies on page 60, but they're versatile and well suited for use with any of the cookies in this book.

Use a *cooling rack* if your cookie output is greater than your supply of baking sheets. Transfer the cookies with an offset spatula onto the cooling rack so you can get the next batch of cookies into the oven.

Parchment paper, *disposable bakery pan liners*, or *aluminum foil* serve a number of purposes. They will keep cookies from sticking to the baking sheets and keep your pans clean in the process. When you use "fine line" decorating or outlining, make a parchment paper cone as shown on page 18. I often use parchment paper in this book to protect the work surface during the decorating phase, and you may find this to be a useful practice, too. Simply transfer the cookies to the parchment paper after they're cool.

To work with royal icing, a *pastry bag* and *tips* are ideal. Pastry tips, like cookie cutters, are available in numerous variations, and each tip is designed for a certain decorating technique. If you want to start with just a few tips, I recommend a star or rosette tip, a small round, a larger round, a rose tip, and a leaf tip. These few tips can be used for many techniques, as you'll see demonstrated in the cookie designs.

Cloth or nylon pastry bags are good, heavy-duty decorating tools. They're easy to refill and last a long time when cleaned properly after each use; simply scrub lightly with warm water and dish detergent and allow to air-dry before storing. A *coupler attachment* allows you to change decorating tips while you're working, and it's compatible with either type of pastry bag. Couplers are inexpensive and an absolute must if you want to use more than one tip while decorating with the same color. The coupler unscrews at the end of the bag, releasing the tip. Then, simply switch the tips and tighten the coupler to lock the new tip in place.

Disposable pastry bags are also available for one-time use; they're good when you're decorating with several colors and they make cleanup a breeze.

Paintbrushes are used in several projects to brush chocolates onto baked cookies.

Lastly, a pair of *scissors* is handy for a number of uses in the kitchen, and you can also cut the unbaked cookies for a unique decorating touch.

Using the Recipes

The recipes are listed on pages 20–24. Just four simple dough recipes were used to create virtually every cookie in this book. (A couple of specialty projects, the fortune cookie and the almond florentine, have recipes listed with the project instructions.) To make your artful decorating even easier, there are only four recipes for the decorative glazes and icings.

You'll note that a yield for the basic recipe is listed on the recipe pages, while the individual project instructions will give specific information for each design. You may get more, or fewer, cookies from the projects than the basic recipe will yield; the sizes in the designs vary. And, the project instructions will also list a suggested baking time for that particular cookie, so be sure to use the time listed for the specific design you're preparing. Again, bear in mind that these are guidelines, as oven temperatures vary.

The design instructions also list a preferred recipe, but you can use almost any type of dough, including the chocolate variations, for any of the cookies. Because the linzer dough contains ground nuts, it has a coarse texture and thus may not be as suitable for some of the more intricate decorating techniques. Read each recipe and let your personal taste be the ultimate guide.

Now, turn the page to see examples of my decorating techniques.

Illustrated Techniques

Here are the basic techniques that I use in decorating beautiful cookies. As you'll see, these methods are easy to master. If you're new to cookie decorating, remember to practice a bit before you begin your first project.

Making and Using a Parchment Paper Cone

To decorate with liquid chocolate glaze, you'll need to use a paper cone, with its tiny opening. It's easy to make and takes just a few steps, as shown in the sequence of photos at the right.

To begin, fold a piece of parchment paper to create a triangle. Flatten the edge thoroughly with a knife. Now, cut the triangle out of the larger piece of paper.

To make the cone, bring one point from the base of the triangle up to the top point. Next, wrap the other base point around and up to the back of the top point.

As shown at the top of the column at the far right, shuffle the paper so the inside piece is tightening while the outer piece wraps. A tight tip should form as you wrap the cone. To complete it, fold in the edges at the top of the cone to hold the shape.

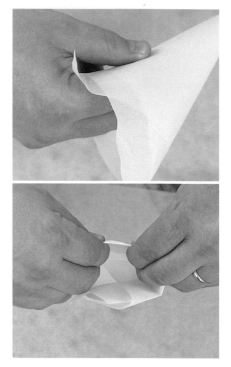

Piping with the Parchment Paper Cone

To fill your cone, hold the edges as you spoon in chocolate glaze or color flow, as shown in the column at the left on page 19. Fold and roll the top over. To pipe with the cone, apply pressure toward the rear of the bag. Make an outline and fill in each portion of the design, as shown in the middle photo of that same column. After you've flooded the design with colored glaze or color flow, you can trace your original outline again, if desired.

While the piping cone also allows you to set your creativity free, there are some traditional decorating designs used in *The Artful Cookie* that are illustrated in the bottom photo of the column below. In the photo, at top right, is an example of Carnegie lace, a delicate embellishment for a special cookie. In the center is a line of piped beads, and at the bottom you'll see a technique called draping, an elegant finishing touch for any design. Use the other examples for inspiration. A quick working tip: use your free hand to steady your piping hand for these techniques.

Applying the Chocolate Glaze

I use several different methods to apply the chocolate glazes to the faces of the cookies. The first is to simply dip the cookie into the melted chocolate, as shown below; give it a gentle shake to remove the excess. A little drip on the edge of the cookie is to be expected. Depending upon the project instructions, you may need to let the cookie set before you continue.

A couple of the designs need a specialized dipping technique, where only part of the cookie is decorated. Here is one example, shown at the bottom of this column, where only the flowers, and not the stems, are dipped in the chocolate.

Finally, when you want to make a precise application of glaze, use a paintbrush, as in the photo at the top of the column at the right.

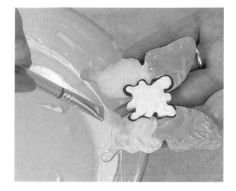

Using the Pastry Bag

To decorate with royal icing, use a pastry bag, as shown below. To fill it, fold the bag upside down and pull the edges back over your wrist. Add the icing as desired and twist it to seal it. Use your thumb and forefinger to control the bag; use your free hand to steady your piping hand, if necessary.

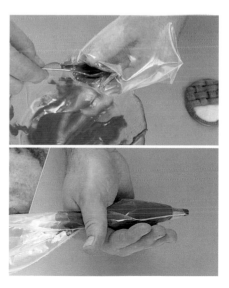

The Artful Recipes

CHOCOLATE VARIATION: To make an entire batch of chocolate dough, substitute ½ cup of cocoa powder for ½ cup of the flour in the recipe; use 2 cups of flour and ½ cup cocoa powder. Unsweetened chocolate bars also can be melted and added to plain shortbread dough to make chocolate dough.

SUBSTITUTIONS: Other flavor extracts can be used instead of vanilla, and all-purpose flour can be substituted for the cake flour.

Shortbread

Yield: 56 cookies
Bake at 350°F for 10–12 minutes

The egg yolks and cake flour make this a rich, light cookie. This dough is more likely to "puff" when baking, which may slightly alter its final shape. Shortbread offers great taste and texture.

1 c butter
½ c granulated sugar
2 tsp vanilla extract
3 large egg yolks
2½ c sifted cake flour

1. Cream the butter, sugar, and vanilla extract.

2. Blend in the egg yolks.

3. Add the flour, mixing only until combined.

4. Refrigerate to set. Keep the dough wrapped to avoid drying the surface.

Sugar Cookie

Yield: 56 cookies
Bake at 350°F for 10–12 minutes

While it's very similar to shortbread, the sugar dough is more stable to work with, as it holds its shape very well.

1 c butter
½ c granulated sugar
2 tsp vanilla extract
1 beaten egg
2½ c all-purpose flour

1. Cream the butter, sugar, and vanilla extract.

2. Blend in the beaten egg.

3. Add the flour, mixing only until combined.

4. Refrigerate to set. Keep the dough wrapped to avoid drying the surface.

CHOCOLATE VARIATION: Follow the directions for the shortbread recipe.

SUBSTITUTION: Other flavor extracts can be used instead of vanilla.

Linzer Cookies
Yield: 68 cookies
Bake at 350°F for 8–10 minutes

Linzer is the classical name for hazelnut sugar dough. The ground hazelnuts create a more unrefined texture than the other recipes, yet this cookie is still utterly delicious.

1 c butter
¾ c granulated sugar
1 Tbsp ground cinnamon
1 tsp baking powder
1 Tbsp vanilla extract
1 egg
2½ c all-purpose flour
1 c finely ground hazelnuts

1. Cream the butter, sugar, cinnamon, baking powder, and vanilla extract.

2. Add the egg to blend.

3. Add the flour and ground hazelnuts, mixing only until combined.

4. Refrigerate to set. Keep the dough wrapped to avoid drying the surface.

very molasses-y "!"

Gingerbread Cookies
Yield: 32 cookies
Bake at 350°F for 8–10 minutes

If you prefer to make an artsy cookie with zing, use this gingerbread recipe, loaded with spices and sweetened with brown sugar and molasses.

½ c butter
½ c brown sugar
1 tsp baking soda
1 tsp ground cinnamon
1 tsp ground ginger
¼ tsp ground cloves
½ tsp salt
½ c molasses
3 c all-purpose flour
¼ c cold water

1. Cream the butter, sugar, soda, spices, and salt.

2. Blend in the molasses.

3. Add the flour, mixing only until combined.

4. Add the cold water.

5. Refrigerate to set. Keep the dough wrapped to avoid drying the surface.

Dark Chocolate Glaze
Yield: About 1½ cups

2 c semisweet chocolate

1. Chop the chocolate into bits and place it in a microwave-safe bowl. Cook for 1 minute; stir and cook again for 45 seconds to 1 minute.

2. Keep stirring and returning the chocolate to the microwave until melted smooth. Chocolate is delicate, so you must stir well between each cooking session. The more liquid chocolate you have in the bowl, the less time it will need in the microwave. If your microwave allows you to reduce the cooking power, choose this option, although chocolate can be melted successfully on full power—it just requires attention and careful stirring.

COLORED VARIATION: Use chopped white chocolate to create the base glaze, following the directions given above; remember to monitor the white chocolate carefully as it's melting. Then, add *only* a powdered or oil-based food color to reach your desired shade; start with a little bit of color. You can always add more if you want a deeper shade.

NOTE: Don't forget that the chocolate glazes must remain melted while you're decorating. Keep them in a pan of warm water or place them in the oven, also in a pan of water, set to the lowest possible temperature.

Chocolate Ganache
Yield: About 1½ cups

½ c heavy cream
1 tsp butter
1 c dark chocolate, chopped

1. Boil the heavy cream and butter. Remove from the heat.

2. Add the chopped chocolate and stir until smooth.

NOTE: The ganache may need to set first, depending upon the application. The project instructions will give specific directions for the use of ganache. If it has set, and you need liquid ganache, it can also be melted by indirect heat.

Eggnog Ganache
Yield: About 1 cup

¼ c eggnog
¾ c white chocolate, chopped

1. Bring the eggnog to boiling in the microwave.

2. Add the white chocolate and stir until smooth. Return to the microwave for 15-second bursts until smooth, stirring between each interval.

NOTE: See the information about setting in the chocolate ganache recipe.

Royal Icing
Yield: About 1½ cups

1 c 10X powdered sugar
½ tsp cream of tartar
1 egg white

1. Place the sugar and cream of tartar in a mixing bowl. Slowly add the egg white to blend into a smooth mixture.

2. Beat on medium speed for 4 minutes to fluff the icing.

3. Keep the icing covered with damp towels so it remains as airtight as possible.

COLOR FLOW VARIATION: Add food coloring to the royal icing to reach the desired tint. When you've created your chosen color, add additional egg white to reach the desired consistency. Color flow will dry in a matter of hours, depending on its thickness.

One last reminder before you begin: oven temperatures vary. Use the times given as guidelines; start with the shortest suggested increment of time for each recipe. See the individual design instructions for specific details.

Artistic Expressions

Butterscotch Stars

Yields about 96 cookies

These stars will shine brightly on any occasion. The cookie and candy combination is irresistible, so the shimmering creations appeal to all the senses.

YOU WILL NEED

- Sugar cookie recipe (page 21)—chocolate variation
- Star cutters, at least two sizes
- Butterscotch candies, crushed

1. Preheat the oven to 350°F. Roll the dough to ⅛ inch. Cut the cookies with the larger cutter and place them on a foil-lined baking sheet. Using a smaller star cutter, cut and remove the center of each cookie. Use a knife to remove the excess dough if necessary.

2. Bake for 10–12 minutes. Remove the cookies from the oven and fill the cavity of each cookie with crushed butterscotch candy. Return them to the oven until the candy melts clear, approximately 5 minutes.

3. Remove the cookies from the oven and leave them on the foil while they cool completely, as the candy needs time to set.

Postmodern Polka Dots

Yields about 50 cookies

Who would imagine that such a simple design scheme could yield such a splendid result?
These cookies abound with artistry, energy…and chocolate.

YOU WILL NEED

- Sugar cookie recipe (page 21) or shortbread recipe (page 20)

- Large square cutter

- Chocolate glaze recipe (page 24)—dark, white, lavender, and yellow

1. Preheat the oven to 350°F. Roll the dough to ¼ inch. Cut the squares, and then cut each square in half diagonally, from corner to corner. Bake for 10–12 minutes. Allow the cookies to cool.

2. Dip the face of one triangle in white chocolate and the other in dark chocolate. On the white cookies, use a parchment paper cone to pipe dark, lavender, and yellow polka dots. On the dark cookies, pipe white, lavender, and yellow polka dots. To create the effect of the dots melting into the background color, pipe the polka dots immediately after you dip the face of the cookie into the chocolate glaze, before the chocolate sets.

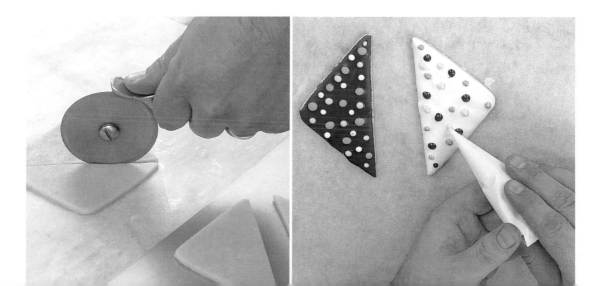

Structural Flowers

Yields about 50 cookies

Like fine architecture, these cookies start with an intriguing design and finish with a flourish.

YOU WILL NEED

- Sugar cookie recipe (page 21) or shortbread recipe (page 20)
- Flower cutter and small round cutter
- Silver dragées
- Chocolate glaze recipe (page 24)—colors of your choice

1. Preheat the oven to 350°F. Roll the dough to ¼ inch. Use the flower cutter to create the body of the cookie. Then, use the round cutter to create the center of each flower; cut five small rounds for the center of each cookie.

2. Place the small rounds in the center of the flower, with the edges touching. Transfer them to a baking sheet after you've constructed the flowers, or simply assemble them directly on the sheet.

3. Press a silver dragée in the center of each small round, and then press a single dragée on each flower petal, approximately 1 inch from the tip. Bake for 10–12 minutes or until slight browning occurs on the edges.

4. After the cookies have cooled, detail them with colored chocolates, using a parchment paper cone.

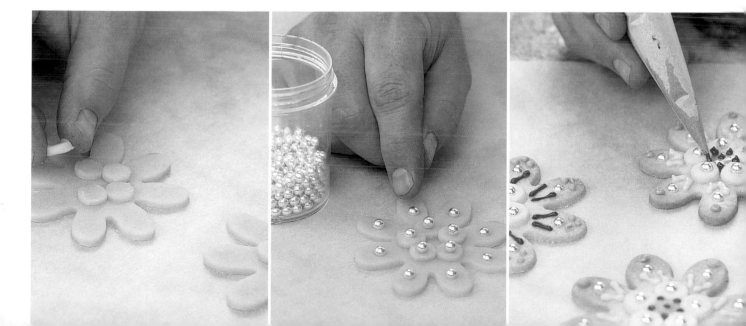

Two-Tone Twists

Yields about 56 cookies

This simple design creates a cookie with panache. Combining the dough recipes produces a scrumptious surprise.

YOU WILL NEED

•Sugar cookie recipe (page 21)—plain and chocolate variation

1. Preheat the oven to 350°F. Use your hands to roll cylinders of both plain and chocolate sugar dough until they're about ½ inch in diameter. The two pieces should also be close to the same length.

2. Now, simply twist together the two lengths. If the dough becomes too soft, it may break during this process, so return it to the refrigerator to chill if necessary.

3. After the twisting is complete, cut the dough into 3-inch lengths and bake for 10–12 minutes, or until set.

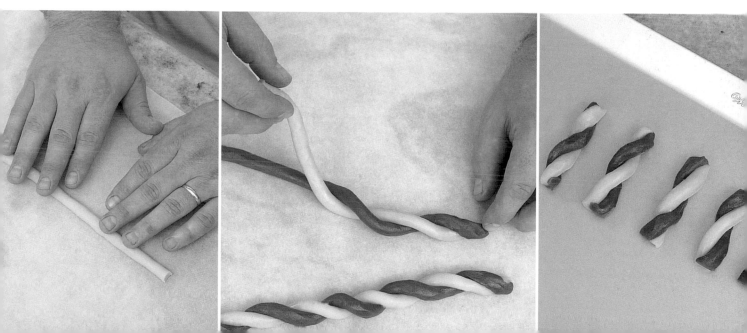

Geometric Shapes

Yields about 72 cookies

This bold collection of cookies is based on simple geometric forms imbued with rich color and adorned with chocolate piping.

YOU WILL NEED

- Sugar cookie recipe (page 21) or shortbread recipe (page 20)
- 1½-inch round cutter
- Clear acrylic ruler or strip
- Chocolate glaze recipe (page 24)— dark and colors of your choice

1. Preheat the oven to 350°F. Roll the dough to ⅛ inch. Cut out the round cookies with the cutter. Cut 1½-inch squares, as well as 1½ x 1¾-inch rectangles, using a pizza cutter. Cut either the squares or the rectangles in half with a paring knife to form the triangles. Bake for 10–12 minutes, then let the cookies cool.

2. Dip the face of each cookie in colored chocolates and allow each to set for a minute or two.

3. Using dark chocolate in a parchment paper cone, pipe lines that echo the shape of the cookie.

Embossed Squares

Yields about 70 cookies

These delicate cookies feature imprinting from several different objects; it's an uncomplicated process that creates subtle texture.

YOU WILL NEED

- Sugar cookie recipe (page 21)—plain and/or chocolate variation
- Square cutter
- Nonstick cooking spray
- Snowflake stamp (or design of your choice)
- Toothpick
- Marzipan sculpting tool with scalloped edge (or similar tool)

1. Preheat the oven to 350°F. Roll the dough to ⅛ inch; cut it with the square cutter and return the cookies to the refrigerator to cool. Warm or soft dough will stick to the stamp in the next step.

2. Lightly spray the stamp of your choice with nonstick cooking spray. Press the stamp into the center of each cookie.

3. Add detail to the cookie by embossing with the toothpick and the marzipan tool, creating a design around the edge of the cookie.

4. Bake for 8–10 minutes. Let the cookies cool.

Tip: These cookies, as well as the stamped cookies on page 88, need to be rolled more thinly than most recipes. The stamped designs are easier to render in a thin cookie, because the detail tends to get lost in thick dough.

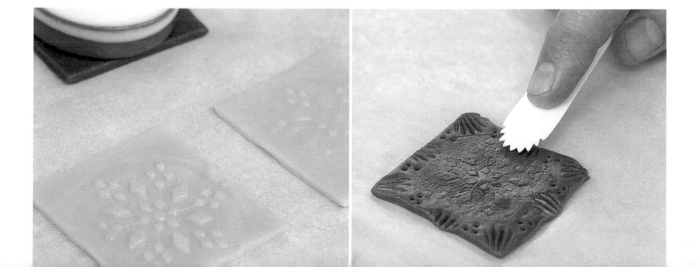

Autumn Leaves

Yields about 70 cookies

Capture the beauty of fall by creating your own vivid leaves from color flow icing. These are meant to be gathered and enjoyed, not tossed by the four winds.

YOU WILL NEED

- Sugar cookie recipe (page 21) or shortbread recipe (20)

- Set of leaf cutters

- Royal icing recipe and color flow variation (page 24)—colors of your choice

- Chocolate glaze recipe (page 24)—white

1. Preheat the oven to 350°F. Roll the dough to ¼ inch. Cut an assortment of leaves and bake them for 10–12 minutes. Let the cookies cool.

2. To decorate with color flow icing, prepare the royal icing recipe. Have a bowl for each color that you plan to use, and separate the icing into these containers.

3. Use liquid food colors for the color flow, although you can use a little chocolate syrup to create brown, if desired. Thin the colors with additional egg white, and then dip the face of each cookie into the desired color. Gently shake away the excess icing.

4. Apply dots to the cookies in a pattern resembling the spine of a leaf, using a parchment paper cone filled with white chocolate glaze. The cookies will need to sit for several hours while the color flow sets.

Variation: You can also create the decorative dots with royal icing and a pastry bag with a small, plain tip.

Spring Flower Basket

Yields about 48 cookies

Celebrate the glory of springtime with these lovely cookies, decorated with royal icing flowers. Plan an unhurried afternoon to weave the baskets.

YOU WILL NEED

- Sugar cookie recipe (page 21)—plain and chocolate variation, if desired
- 2½-inch oval cutter
- Pastry brush
- Water
- Marzipan sculpting tool with scalloped edge (or similar tool)
- Royal icing recipe (page 24)—colors of your choice

1. Preheat the oven to 350°F. Roll the dough to ⅛ inch. Cut out the cookies with the oval cutter.

2. With the pizza cutter, cut several strips that are ⅜ inch wide x 3 inches long. (It's important to have excess when you're working.) Refrigerate the strips for just about 5 minutes, because if they're too warm and soft, they'll fall apart. After refrigeration, they should be pliable enough to weave but not cold enough to break.

3. Brush the ovals with water. Lay the horizontal strips of dough beginning at the bottom of a cookie, covering about 1½ inches of the oval. Peel back every other strip to the edge of the cookie, and lay a vertical strip. Put the horizontal strips back into place. Repeat with the alternate horizontal strips, adding a new vertical strip, until the basket is woven. Trim the excess dough.

4. Cut one strip in half lengthwise and lay it across the upper edge of the cookie to form the handle.

5. Crimp the handle with the sculpting tool to adhere it, as well as to decorate it. If the dough becomes soft while you're working, refrigerate the strips for a little while to firm. The dough needs to be pliable enough to bend while working, however, so don't chill them for too long.

6. Bake for 10–12 minutes. Let the cookies cool.

7. Make colorful flowers and leaves from royal icing, using a pastry bag and decorating tips such as a leaf tip, a rose tip, a drop star, and a round tip. The icing will set in a couple of hours.

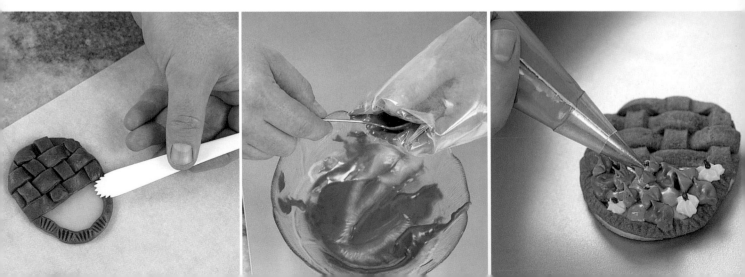

A Short Sweet History

We've long enjoyed scrumptious little baked goods that we now call cookies.

Greeks and Romans ate small cakes that were the ancestors of today's cookies. The Persians may have eaten early cookies, too, perhaps even sweetened with sugar. Gradually, other ingredients such as fruits, nuts, and spices were added to these little cakes. As baking methods evolved through the centuries, regional specialties developed throughout Europe: the Italians were particularly adept, creating pizzelles, biscotti, and macaroons, among others. Immigrants from other countries—the English, the Scotch, and the Dutch, in particular—brought their recipes to the United States during the colonial period.

In fact, settlers from Holland popularized the word "cookie" in America. It derives from the Dutch *koekje*, which translates as "little cake." The derivation of the word appears to be thus: Way back when baking was done in a primitive oven, on a hearth, or over coals, a *koekje*–a little cake–was baked from a small amount of batter to test the heat of the oven. The *koekje* evolved into a "cookie" and became a baked item in and of itself, retaining its endearing name.

As reliable home ovens became commonplace and leavenings such as baking powder became available, cookie baking became a sensation. Many of our favorite cookie recipes, such as oatmeal, peanut butter, brownie, and chocolate chip, have been created within the last 100 years or so.

Classy Checkerboards

Yields about 56 cookies

These graphic cookies result from easy cutting and stacking. Present them on a sleek modern plate for a stylish delight.

YOU WILL NEED

- Sugar cookie recipe (page 21)—plain and chocolate variation, or shortbread recipe (page 20)—plain and chocolate variation
- Mini loaf pan
- Pastry brush
- Water

1. Mold individual bricks of both plain and chocolate dough in the mini loaf pan. Press the soft dough to ¾ inch for each brick. Make two chocolate bricks and two plain bricks, for a total of four.

2. Brush the top of each brick with water to fuse as you stack these bricks alternately. Refrigerate to set.

3. Cut strips of dough from top to bottom that are each ½ inch thick; there should be three strips. Lay the first strip down and brush it with water. Place the next strip on top of the first, but in reverse orientation, so the plain and chocolate alternate. Brush it with water and add the final strip.

4. Preheat the oven to 350°F. Refrigerate the dough to set. Slice the cookies ½ inch thick and bake for 10–12 minutes.

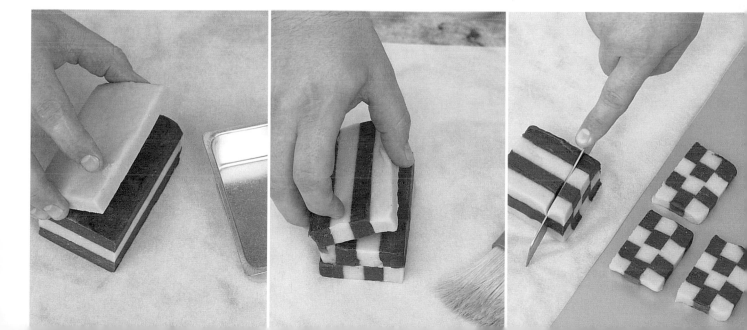

Mondrian's Cookies

Yields about 70 cookies

In the spirit of the famed painter, these cookies boast bold lines of color complemented by the twinkle of silver dragées.

YOU WILL NEED

- Sugar cookie recipe (page 21) or shortbread recipe (page 20)
- Oval cutter
- Chocolate glaze recipe (page 24)—white, dark, and the colors of your choice
- Silver dragées

1. Preheat the oven to 350°F. Roll the dough to ¼ inch. Cut out the cookies with the oval cutter and bake them for 10–12 minutes. Allow them to cool.

2. Dip the face of each cookie in the white chocolate glaze, immediately sprinkle on the dragées, and let the cookies set for a few moments.

3. Apply the colored chocolates by making lines with a parchment paper cone, and then fill in the outlined areas. Have fun as you create these designs! To finish, outline the colored lines with dark chocolate.

Alternatives: You can create a completely different cookie by adapting this basic idea. Create a stencil from strips of paper, drape it over the cookie, and sprinkle the surface with powdered sugar, colored powder, or cinnamon.

Tip: If necessary, use the final dark chocolate outlines to "straighten" any errant color blocks.

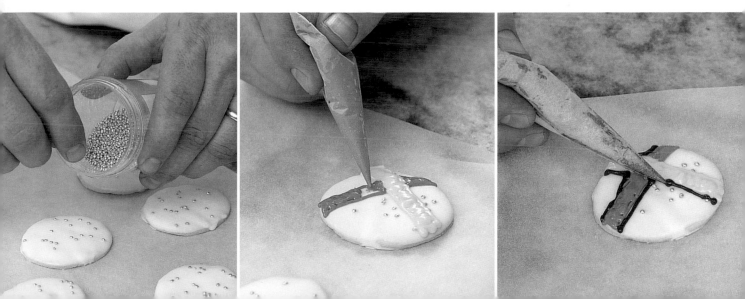

Frosted Flowers

Yields about 50 cookies

As if kissed by the morning dew, these cookies sparkle from a coating of colored sugar.

YOU WILL NEED

- Sugar cookie recipe (page 21) or shortbread recipe (page 20)
- Medium round cutter and small flower cutter
- Granulated sugar
- Reclosable plastic bags
- Powdered food coloring—colors of your choice
- Small bowls (some for sugar and some for water)
- Paper towels

1. Preheat the oven to 350°F. Roll the dough to ¼ inch. For each flower, cut six round cookies for the petals. Then, use the small flower cutter to make the centers for each cookie.

2. Color the sugar to decorate the petals, using ⅛ cup of granulated sugar for each color. (The cookies shown here are decorated with gradated shades of the same color.) Place the sugar in a reclosable plastic bag, add the desired amount of food coloring, and shake to blend. Empty the sugar into a small bowl.

3. Dip approximately one-third of each petal into the bowl of water, pat the excess on a paper towel, and dip it into the colored sugar. Repeat for the other five round petals.

4. Assemble the flowers on a baking sheet by overlapping each petal, placing each successive petal on the undecorated portion of the previous one. Tuck the last petal under the first petal, using a knife or spatula if necessary. To complete the embellishment, dip the small flowers into the water, pat off the excess, and dip the faces into a sugar of contrasting color. Place in the center of each cookie.

5. Bake for 10–12 minutes. Let the cookies cool.

Fluttering Butterflies

Yields about 56 cookies

These fanciful butterflies are beautiful enough to collect, just like their natural counterparts.

YOU WILL NEED

- Sugar cookie recipe (page 21) or shortbread recipe (page 20)
- Butterfly cutters, at least 2 sizes
- Chocolate glaze recipe (page 24)—dark and colors of your choice
- Paintbrush

1. Preheat the oven to 350°F. Roll the dough to ¼ inch.

2. To make the large cookies, cut with the larger butterfly cutter. Use the smaller cutter to gently press into the center of each cookie to mark it for decorating. Bake for 10–12 minutes. Let the cookies cool.

3. Using a parchment paper cone, outline the center impression with dark chocolate, and fill in the center with the color of your choice.

4. Use a paintbrush to color the upper wings of the butterfly; let the chocolate set before you brush on the second color. Add finishing details with piping as desired.

5. For the small butterflies, dip the face of each cookie in a colored chocolate glaze. Detail with piping as desired.

Stylish Occasions

Array of Gifts

Yields about 56 cookies

These festive delights are an imaginative substitute for a birthday cake. They also give you ample opportunity for creativity with the wrapping.

YOU WILL NEED

- Sugar cookie recipe (page 21) or shortbread recipe (page 20)

- Assorted cutters

- Chocolate glaze recipe (page 24)—colors of your choice

- Embellishments, such as dragées

1. Preheat the oven to 350°F. Roll the dough to ¼ inch. Use a variety of cutters to create an assortment of cookies. Bake for 10–12 minutes. Let the cookies cool.

2. Dip the faces of the cookies in the various colored chocolates. Then, using a parchment paper cone, pipe latticework, ribbons, and bows to decorate. If you embellish with dragées, be sure to add them when the chocolate is still wet so they adhere to the surface.

Tip: You can also use royal icing, or even candies, to detail these cookies.

Valentine Hearts

Yields about 56 cookies

You'll woo any sweetheart with these delectable valentines. Choose your preferred style,
or make a combination for an irresistible offering.

- Sugar cookie recipe (page 21) or shortbread recipe (page 20)—plain and chocolate variations, if desired

- Heart cutters, in two sizes

- Chocolate glaze recipe (page 24)—dark, white, and pink

- Toothpick

1. Preheat the oven to 350°F. Roll the plain dough to ¼ inch. Cut out the hearts with the larger cutter.

2. To create the two-toned cookies, use the smaller cutter to remove the center of the hearts you cut in step 1. Roll a batch of chocolate dough to ¼ inch. Now, cut some of the smaller hearts from the chocolate dough and insert them in the center of the plain hearts. Bake for 10–12 minutes, and then let the cookies cool.

3. To embellish these cookies, put white chocolate glaze in a parchment paper cone and write "Be Mine" (or the beguiling phrase of your choice) on the chocolate heart. Pipe dark chocolate beading over the seam between the inner and outer hearts.

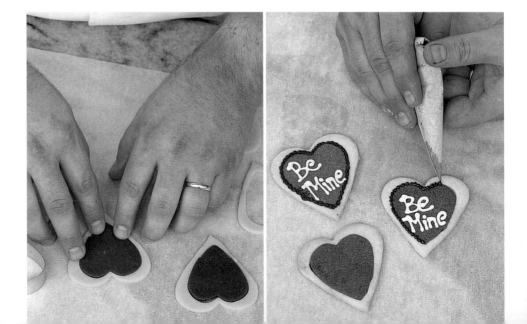

4. To make the pink hearts, dip the face of each cookie in pink glaze. Working while the pink chocolate is still wet, pipe three dots of dark chocolate in the center of the cookie. Quickly drag a toothpick through the middle of each dot to create the heart effect; this must be done before the dark chocolate sets. To finish, pipe white chocolate beading around the outline of each cookie.

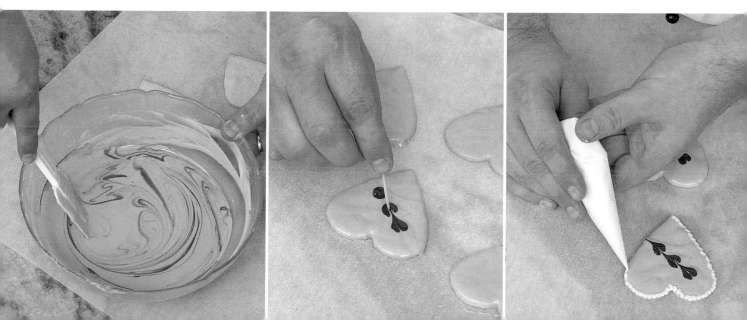

Flat Gingerbread House

Yields about 32 cookies

Here's a beautiful creation without the structural concerns of a complete gingerbread house. The warm glow through the windows adds true holiday cheer.

YOU WILL NEED

- Gingerbread recipe (page 23)
- Cardboard
- Pencil
- Scissors or craft knife
- Basket weave stamp
- Round cutter and oval cutter
- Hard candies, crushed
- Royal icing recipe (page 24)

1. Preheat the oven to 350°F. Make a basic house template out of the cardboard.

2. Roll the gingerbread dough to ¼ inch, and trim it to have a straight edge. Place the template on this straight edge and use it for a guide as you cut out the house with a pizza cutter. Emboss the house with the basket weave tool, and then make the windows with the cutters.

3. Use a paring knife to create the door, making a series of short cuts so you don't stretch the dough. The door opening needs to stay square, and be sure that you don't cut it all the way to the bottom of the dough, so the shape of the cookie remains stable.

4. Bake for 10–12 minutes. Remove from the oven. Spoon the crushed hard candy into the door and window openings. Return the gingerbread to the oven until the candy melts clear, approximately 5 minutes.

5. Once the flat gingerbread house has cooled, use a pastry bag with a small star tip and a small plain tip to add royal icing borders.

Good Fortune Cookies

Yields about 24 cookies

Ensure good luck when you make personalized fortune cookies; a quick fold and twist are all you need to make an artful change in someone's life.

YOU WILL NEED
- Plastic can lid (or similar piece of plastic)
- Craft knife or scissors
- Silicone baking mat
- Nonstick cooking spray
- Fortunes

BATTER
- ¼ c 10X powdered sugar
- ½ tsp butter
- ¼ c all-purpose flour
- 1 egg white
- ¼ tsp lemon extract

1. Make a circular form to shape the cookies; it doesn't have to be too polished. An easy method is to use a thin plastic lid from a large can; cut out a 4-inch circle in the middle.

2. Preheat the oven to 400°F. Make the batter for the cookies. Cream the sugar and butter, and then add the flour. Slowly add the egg white, blending it into the dry mixture. Finally, add the lemon extract. Use the batter immediately.

3. Bake the cookies on a silicone baking mat, available from a specialty kitchen store. Lightly spray the baking mat with non-stick cooking spray. Put a small amount of batter in the center of your form and use a small offset spatula to spread it to the edges of the circle. Remove the form. (Because the cookies must be shaped while hot from the oven, don't bake more than six at a time.) Bake for 8–10 minutes or until lightly browned on the edges.

4. Shape the cookies quickly. Pick up each cookie with the offset spatula and place a fortune in the center. Fold each cookie to form a half moon.

5. Fold the cookies again, so the points touch one another. If the cookies set too fast, return them briefly to the oven to soften.

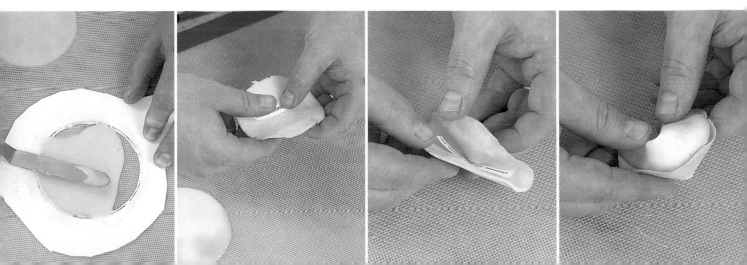

Holiday Wreath

Yields about 56 cookies

Here's an edible decoration for the holidays. These colorful wreaths convey the spirit of the season.

YOU WILL NEED

- Sugar cookie recipe (page 21) or shortbread recipe (page 20)
- Green food coloring
- Rose leaf cutter
- Marker
- Cup or glass
- Chocolate glaze recipe (page 24)—white
- Cinnamon dots

1. Preheat the oven to 350°F. Add the green food color to the dough as you're mixing, but reserve a tiny portion of plain dough. Roll the green dough to ⅛ inch. Using a small rose leaf cutter, cut several leaves. From the remaining plain dough, fashion a bow in an hourglass shape. Set the bow aside.

2. Trace around the edge of a cup or glass to form a circle on a piece of aluminum foil. Place the leaves along the outline, slightly overlapping them. Use the knife to lift the first leaf over the last one in the circle. Add the bow. Bake on the foil for 12–15 minutes.

3. After the cookies have cooled, use a parchment paper cone to pipe a white chocolate ribbon below the bow. Decorate with cinnamon candies; first add a dab of chocolate glaze, and then place the cinnamon dots on top.

Minted Tea(pot) Cookies

Yields about 30 cookies

These refreshing treats are perfect for afternoon tea or any other genteel occasion when a dainty morsel is de rigueur.

YOU WILL NEED

- Sugar cookie recipe (page 21) or shortbread recipe (page 20)
- Teapot cutter (and round cutters with scalloped edges, if desired)
- Mint jelly
- Hand sifter
- Circular plastic canvas (from a craft store)
- Powdered sugar

1. Preheat the oven to 350°F. Roll the dough to ⅛ inch. Use the cutter(s) to shape the cookies. Punch three small holes in a triangle pattern on half of the cookies, which will be the tops; save the other half of the cookies for the bottoms. A plain pastry tip works quite well to punch small, consistent holes. (If you also wish to make the round cookies, use a smaller cutter to remove the centers.) Bake for 10–12 minutes. Allow the cookies to cool.

2. Use mint jelly for the filling. First, stir the jelly to smooth. Then spread a thin amount of jelly on the bottom of each cookie, but don't spread it all the way to the edges. Make the jelly a little thicker in the middle.

3. To create the pattern on top, place the plastic canvas on top of each cookie and sift powdered sugar onto it *before* covering the bottom. Carefully remove the plastic canvas. Because of the delicate nature of this procedure, it may be difficult to get a perfect pattern each time. You'll find that a light dusting of sugar leaves a better design.

4. Press the tops to the bottoms. Jelly should be visible through the holes in the top of each cookie.

Tip: Because a sandwich-style treat such as this one needs two cookies (one for the top and one for the bottom), roll the dough a little thinner.

Alternative: Use apricot jam in some of the cookies, too, for a nice color contrast and refined presentation.

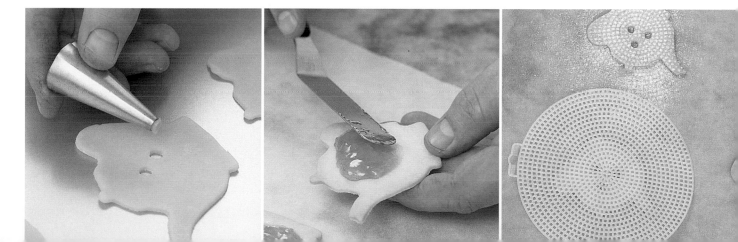

Baby Shower Bears

Yields about 36 cookies

Transcend the ordinary with these refined cookies that celebrate a new arrival. The baby bear within contains luscious chocolate ganache.

YOU WILL NEED

- Sugar cookie recipe (page 21) or shortbread recipe (page 20)
- Bear cutters (large and small)
- Chocolate glaze recipe (page 24)—dark, pink, and blue
- Chocolate ganache recipe (page 24)

1. Preheat the oven to 350°F. Roll the dough to ¼ inch and cut out the bears with the large cutter. Transfer the cookies to a baking sheet and use the small cutter to make the baby bear cutouts. Bake for 10–12 minutes and let the cookies cool.

2. Dip the bear in pink or blue chocolate, as desired.

3. Fill each cutout with melted chocolate ganache, using a parchment paper cone.

4. To finish, use a parchment paper cone to outline each bear with the dark chocolate glaze. Let the ganache and glaze set.

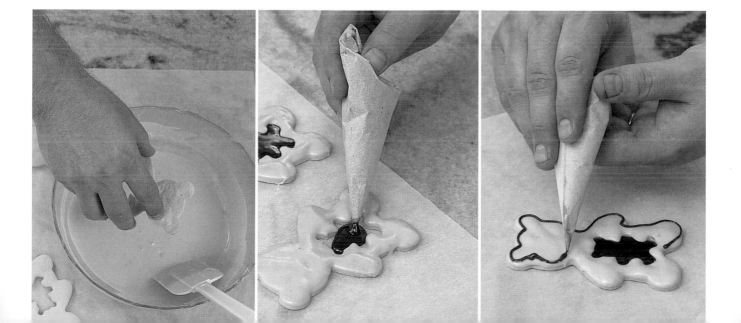

Coconut Easter Eggs

Yields about 70 cookies

Colored coconut lends a textured look that resembles the grass in an Easter basket. Children young and old will enjoy these cheerful cookies.

YOU WILL NEED

- Sugar cookie recipe (page 21) or shortbread recipe (page 20)
- Oval cutter
- ¼ c coconut
- Reclosable plastic bag
- Food coloring—colors of your choice
- Chocolate glaze recipe (page 24)—white
- Jellybeans—colors of your choice

1. Preheat the oven to 350°F. Roll the dough to ¼ inch. Cut out the oval cookies and bake for 10–12 minutes, or until slightly brown. Allow the cookies to cool.

2. Put the coconut in the plastic bag. Add a few drops of food coloring, seal it tightly, and shake the bag to distribute the color throughout the coconut. More food coloring can be added to reach the desired shade. Repeat for as many colors as desired.

3. Dip the face of each cookie in the white chocolate glaze, and then immediately dip each into the coconut. Lightly shake off any excess coconut.

4. Using a parchment paper cone, pipe on a dab of white chocolate, and then place a jellybean on top.

Tip: Try coloring each half of the egg a different color. Or use a slender stripe of dragées for a luminous adornment.

Sparkling Snowflakes

Yields about 72 cookies

A simply elegant creation, these stunning snowflakes pair white chocolate glaze and coarse sugar to exquisite effect.

YOU WILL NEED

- Sugar cookie recipe (page 21) or shortbread recipe (page 20)
- Snowflake cutters
- Chocolate glaze recipe (page 24)—white
- Coarse sugar

1. Preheat the oven to 350°F. Roll the dough to ¼ inch. Cut out the cookies with the snowflake cutters.

2. Bake for 10–12 minutes. Once the cookies are cool, dip the faces in white chocolate and sprinkle them with coarse sugar immediately, before the chocolate sets.

Fluted Gingerbread Cups

Yields about 100 cookies

These elegant holiday treats provide a delicate crunch that complements the rich eggnog filling.
The ginger will linger on the palate, making the indulgence all the more memorable.

YOU WILL NEED

- Gingerbread recipe (page 23)

- Nonstick mini muffin pan

- 2-inch round cutter

- Eggnog ganache recipe (page 24)—five
  times the basic recipe

1. Preheat the oven to 350°F. Lightly grease the muffin pan.

2. Roll the gingerbread dough very thin for this recipe, approximately ⅛ inch. Using the round cutter, cut 12 pieces.

3. Delicately work the round pieces into the muffin cups, being careful not to tear the dough. The gingerbread rounds should be slightly bigger than the openings in the pan. Press the dough into the bottom of each cup and allow the rim to gently fold.

4. Bake for 10–12 minutes. Allow the cups to cool in the pan.

5. Prepare the eggnog ganache. Use a parchment paper cone to fill the tartlets. Let the ganache set.

Bride and Groom

Yields about 60 cookies

These are delicious mementos for an unforgettable day. Use chocolates to decorate an elegant pair of cookies in honor of the newlyweds.

YOU WILL NEED

• Sugar cookie recipe (page 21) or shortbread recipe (page 20)

• Oval cookie cutter

• Chocolate glaze recipe (page 24)—white and dark

1. Preheat the oven to 350°F. Roll the dough to ¼ inch and cut the oval cookies. Bake for 10–12 minutes and let them cool.

2. Dip the face of each cookie in a bowl of white chocolate glaze. Allow the chocolate to set before continuing.

3. To create the bride, use a parchment paper cone to pipe white chocolate into a V for the neckline. Then, pipe a row of dots to simulate a strand of pearls. Pipe the body in Carnegie lace; this is a series of curls and twists that's a freehand technique. See the illustrated techniques on page 18.

4. To decorate the groom, use the cookies that have already been dipped in white chocolate glaze. Dip one side of the cookie into the dark chocolate glaze, then rotate it and dip the second side at the opposite angle, leaving the white chocolate triangle for a vest. You'll be covering part of the dark chocolate from the first dip with that from the second.

5. Pipe a bow tie with dark chocolate, making an outline that resembles an hourglass on its side. Fill in the outline with dark chocolate and apply chocolate dots for buttons.

The Lure of Chocolate

Chocolate has held us in its spell for centuries. Christopher Columbus brought cocoa beans, a product of the New World, to Spain when he returned from his exploration of North America. Their potential was unrecognized until the early sixteenth century when Hernando Cortez found the Aztecs drinking liquid chocolate; rather than the sweet beverage we adore today, it was a bitter drink, mixed with spices and chili peppers.

The enterprising Spanish sweetened the concoction and it became a drink of the aristocracy, yet the Spaniards somehow managed to keep the secrets of the trade to themselves for almost a century. Then, after the production techniques were revealed, chocolate houses spread throughout Europe, though the high price insured that only the elite could partake of the treasured elixir. Mechanization of the grinding process, first by the steam engine, then by the cocoa press, soon made chocolate available to all.

Once the domain of the Spanish, other countries made significant contributions to the development of chocolate in all its irresistible forms. The English introduced bars and the Swiss developed milk chocolate. Belgian chocolatiers elevated the process to a high art, producing divine confections both luscious and lovely. Back in the New World, home of the cocoa bean, chocolate production in the United States began in the late 1700s.

Although it's an important (some may say integral) ingredient in many cookies today, chocolate took its sweet time finding its way into a popular recipe. Brownies, the rich gooey bar cookies, first appeared in American cookbooks in the early 1900s, though the precise origin of the recipe is unknown. One of the most notable innovations involving both cookie and chocolate occurred in Massachusetts in 1930, when Ruth Wakefield, proprietor of the Toll House Inn, experimented by adding bits of chocolate to a traditional butter cookie recipe. The result—the now-ubiquitous chocolate chip cookie—has become an international favorite.

Creative Indulgences

Decorated Pinwheels

Yields about 56 cookies

The pièce de résistance of these whirling confections is the heavenly white chocolate decoration on each point.

YOU WILL NEED

- •Sugar cookie recipe (page 21) or shortbread recipe (page 20)
- •Square cutter
- •Bake-proof jam and/or chocolate drops
- •Chocolate glaze recipe (page 24) — white

1. Preheat the oven to 350°F. Roll the dough into a ¼-inch thick rectangle and cut it into squares. On each square, use a paring knife to cut each of the four points halfway to the center of the square.

2. Fold the dough on one side of each cut, bringing the point to the center of the cookie. Use a paring knife to lift each piece, if necessary.

3. Fill the centers with bake-proof jam or add chocolate drops. Transfer the cookies to a baking sheet.

4. Bake for 10–12 minutes, or until the points of each pinwheel are lightly brown.

5. Once the cookies have cooled, dip each point of the pinwheel into the white chocolate glaze. Garnish with white chocolate piping, using a parchment paper cone.

Crimped Apricot Pockets

Yields about 72 cookies

These pockets are filled with jam, then decorated with piping and a delicate dusting of powdered sugar. The result is a graceful pastry.

YOU WILL NEED

- Sugar cookie recipe (page 21) or shortbread recipe (page 20)
- 2-inch round cookie cutter
- Bake-proof apricot jam
- Water or beaten egg
- Pastry brush
- Marzipan sculpting tool with scalloped edge (or similar tool)
- Chocolate glaze recipe (page 24)—dark
- Confectioners' sugar

1. Preheat the oven to 350°F. Roll the dough to ¼ inch, and then cut out the cookies.

2. Spoon bake-proof apricot jam into the center. Fold over and brush with a little water or egg, then seal to create a pocket. Crimp along the edge with the marzipan sculpting tool.

3. To allow steam to escape, cut the top of each pocket with scissors. If you're working on parchment paper, transfer the cookies to a baking sheet. Bake for 10–12 minutes.

4. When cool, use a parchment paper cone to stripe with dark chocolate. Lightly dust with confectioners' sugar to finish.

Tip: The tines of a fork work very well as a crimping tool, too.

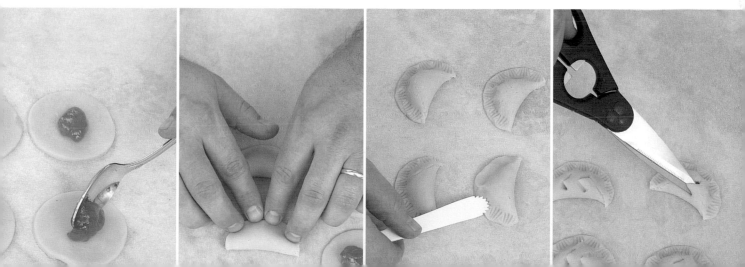

Chocolate Chip Macaroons

Yields about 42 cookies

This unique rolled macaroon is a variation on classic European recipes. Coconut and chocolate are irresistible, *non?*

YOU WILL NEED
- Double boiler
- Sugar cookie recipe (page 21)— chocolate variation
- Plastic wrap

FILLING
- 2¾ c coconut
- 6 egg whites
- 1 c granulated sugar
- 3 Tbsp cornstarch
- ¾ c mini chocolate chips

1. Prepare the macaroon filling by cooking together in a double boiler the coconut, egg whites, sugar, and cornstarch until thick. Cool the filling completely in the refrigerator, then fold in the mini chocolate chips. (If the filling is not cool, the chips will melt when you blend them into the mixture.) Place the filling in a length of plastic wrap and roll into a cylinder approximately 1 inch in diameter. Freeze until firm.

2. Roll out the chocolate dough into a rectangle approximately 3 inches wide x 8 inches long. Add the cylinder of macaroon and roll. Trim the excess dough. Refrigerate until the dough is firm and set.

3. Preheat the oven to 375°F. Slice the dough into ½-inch cookies, using a chef's knife. If the dough breaks and cracks while slicing, allow it to soften a little. Space the cookies ½ inch apart on the baking sheet.

4. Bake for 12–15 minutes or until the macaroon starts to color and is spongy.

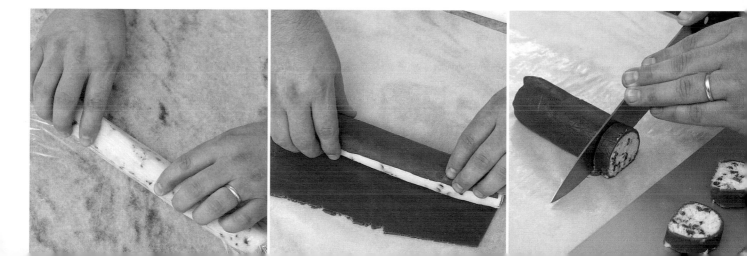

Garden of Tulips

Yields about 64 cookies

Assemble an enchanting edible bouquet with the flowers you create using these specialty cutters.

YOU WILL NEED

- Sugar cookie recipe (page 21) or shortbread recipe (page 20)
- Tulip cutters
- Chocolate glaze recipe (page 24)— green, plus additional colors of your choice
- Paintbrush

1. Preheat the oven to 350°F. Roll the dough to ¼ inch. Cut out the tulips, then bake for 10–12 minutes. Let the cookies cool.

2. Dip the upper face of each cookie in the colored glaze. Let each cookie set.

3. Brush the leaves and the stem of each cookie with green glaze. Let the chocolate set.

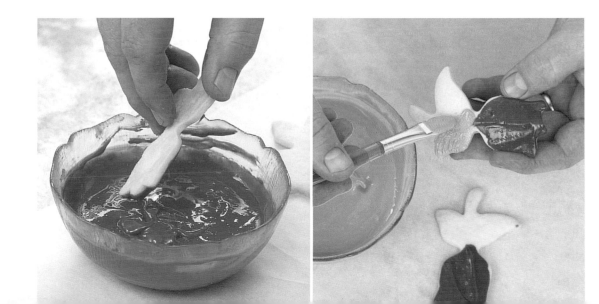

Peanut (Butter) & Jelly Spirals

Yields about 48 cookies

This resplendent swirl of jam and nuts begs to be savored; it's a sophisticated version of everyone's favorite sandwich.

YOU WILL NEED

- Sugar cookie recipe (page 21) or shortbread recipe (page 20)
- Raspberry jam
- Chopped peanuts

1. On a piece of parchment paper, roll the dough to ¼ inch, making a rectangle. (If the dough becomes soft during this step, refrigerate it for a few minutes until it's firm.) Spread the raspberry jam evenly over the dough, covering it completely yet thinly.

2. Sprinkle the chopped peanuts over the layer of jam. Use the paper to nudge the edge of the dough and roll it up from the bottom. Freeze to set.

3. Preheat the oven to 350°F. Cut the cookies into ¼-inch disks; if the dough breaks or cracks, allow the roll to soften a bit. Place them ½ inch apart on the cookie sheet and bake for 12–15 minutes.

Stamped Cookies

Yields about 40 cookies

This playful design makes for a pleasurable afternoon of easy baking.

YOU WILL NEED

- Gingerbread recipe (page 23)
- Nonstick cooking spray
- Paper towel
- Stamp of your choice
- Crimped-edge tool, like a ravioli cutter

1. Preheat the oven to 350°F. Roll the dough to ⅛ inch; thinner dough will be better for retaining detail in the image transfer. Return it to the refrigerator to cool. Warm or soft dough will stick to the stamp in the next step.

2. Lightly spray the stamp with nonstick cooking spray. Dab off the excess with a paper towel, so you have a light coating of spray on the stamp. Press the stamp firmly into the dough, capturing the complete image with all details. Slowly and carefully peel off the stamp; you can repair any slight distortions before you bake.

3. Use the crimped-edge tool to cut around the image and form each cookie.

4. Bake for 8–10 minutes. Let the cookies cool.

Tip: Anything with a raised pattern can be used to stamp cookie dough. This project features a blank sun catcher that was purchased at a craft store.

Almond Florentines

Yields about 64 cookies

These cookies don't need decoration to tantalize the taste buds. Almond lovers will delight in these crunchy confections.

YOU WILL NEED

- Sugar cookie recipe (page 21)
- 9 x 13-inch pan
- Candy thermometer

TOPPING

- ½ c granulated sugar
- ½ c butter
- 2 Tbsp honey
- 2 Tbsp milk
- 1½ c slivered almonds, toasted

1. Preheat the oven to 350°F. Roll the dough to ¼ inch, making a 10 x 14-inch rectangle. Line the bottom of the pan with foil (you could also lightly grease the pan with nonstick cooking spray instead, if you prefer). Place the dough into the pan; if it should happen to break during the process, simply press it into the bottom of the pan.

2. Prick the dough with a fork to allow steam to escape and to avoid blisters. Bake for 10–12 minutes or until slight browning occurs on the edges of the cookies.

3. To make the topping, bring the sugar, butter, honey, and milk to a boil. Reduce the heat and cook until the mixture becomes frothy and turns a light caramel color; this should occur at about 230°F on the candy thermometer. Stir in the toasted almonds.

4. Carefully pour the mixture over the baked dough in the pan. Spread the topping evenly over the dough with an offset spatula. Return to the oven at 350°F until the mixture fills the pan and bubbles all over, approximately 5 minutes.

5. Cool until the topping is set. Cut into strips and then cut into triangles.

Marbled Collection

Yields about 56 cookies

These sublime delights are sure to please. Color contrasts and highlights are important when you decorate these cookies.

YOU WILL NEED

- Sugar cookie recipe (page 21) or shortbread recipe (page 20)
- Round cutters
- Chocolate glaze recipe (page 24)— dark, white, and the additional colors of your choice
- Toothpicks

1. Preheat the oven to 350°F. Roll the dough to ¼ inch. Cut out and bake the cookies for 10–12 minutes. Let them cool.

2. Dip the face of each cookie in the appropriate base color, either white or dark glaze. To create the half-dark and half-white cookies, dip one side in dark and the other in white, then swirl the glazes together with an offset spatula before the chocolates set.

3. To make the design on the dark chocolate base, use a parchment paper cone to pipe a circular line of white chocolate that radiates from the center of the cookie. Working quickly while the chocolate is still liquid, use a toothpick to draw through the circle, alternating between beginning in the center of the cookie and drawing out with beginning at the edge and drawing in.

4. To create the design on the white chocolate base, apply the colors in looping lines. Again, working quickly before the chocolates set, use the toothpick to draw through the lines for the length of the cookie, alternating between dragging top to bottom and bottom to top.

Tips: Have several colors of chocolate melted and ready before you begin working. And a warm room is ideal while you're working on these cookies, so the chocolate stays liquid while you're creating the designs. Finally, don't cut too many lines with the toothpicks, or you'll blend the colors too much.

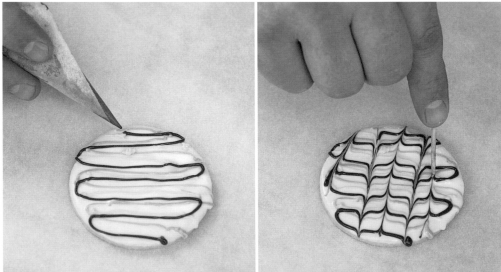

Artful Cookies Around the Globe

We've long appreciated the artistry of bakers throughout the world who have given us splendid cookies to savor. Since the Italians developed so many fabulous cookies, I'll start with them.

Amaretti. This is the classical Italian almond macaroon, crunchy on the outside but soft on the inside. It's also dome-shaped, like its popular coconut cousin. Amaretti were likely created in Italy, during or just after the Renaissance.

Biscotti. In Italian, biscotti means "twice baked." Indeed, these dry cookies, traditionally flavored with anise, are baked twice, which lends them a long shelf life. It's said that Christopher Columbus relied on a form of biscotti during his long voyages. Perhaps biscotti originated in Tuscany a century or so before Columbus's explorations.

Lebkuchen. These holiday cookies, a honey-based treat featuring fruits and nuts, are favorites in Germany; they're likely descendants of the cakes the Romans ate and are cousins to the fruitcake.

Madelaines. Reportedly named for the French pastry chef who created these shell-shaped delights, they are usually flavored with orange or lemon, baked to perfection, and dusted with confectioners' sugar.

Petits Fours. Small elegant treats often featuring a delectable filling, these cookies were baked as the ovens were cooling off after the large goods had been removed. (The name, of course, is French, meaning "small oven.") Petits fours can be made from cookies, cake, marzipan—much can be left to the imagination of the baker. Cookies are in the category called petits fours secs (dry); others are petits fours glacés (iced) or petits fours frais (filled).

Pizzelles. Back to those clever Italians again. Pizzelles are cooked in irons, producing a thin, crisp cookie. Though modern recipes no longer include it, traditional pizzelles called for pork fat in the batter.

Shortbread. What a simple delight these crunchy, buttery cookies are! Adored for centuries, these Scottish classics were once served only during the holiday season. Immigrants likely brought a love for shortbread to the New World.

Springerle. Still a traditional holiday cookie in Austria and beyond, springerle are molded cookies of various designs flavored with anise. Specialized rolling pins are now available to imprint the designs into the cookie dough.

Tuiles. The French have such lyrical names for cookies, don't they? Actually, tuile means "tile" *en français*, because these confections resemble the roofing tiles used in earlier times. Tuiles are shaped while still warm, placed over a rolling pin to achieve their classic draped form.

Strawberry Linzer Leaves

Yields about 40 cookies

These earthy creations are a natural delight, featuring a bounty of nuts and fruit in the hazelnut dough and strawberry filling.

YOU WILL NEED

- Linzer recipe (page 23)
- Oak leaf cookie cutter
- Strawberry jam
- Confectioners' sugar

1. Preheat the oven to 350°F. Roll the dough to ⅛ inch; because this recipe calls for sandwiching, the cookies should be delicate.

2. Cut the dough with the oak leaf cutter. Bake the cookies for 8–10 minutes.

3. After the cookies have cooled, apply a thin layer of strawberry jam with an offset spatula. Attach another cookie for the top.

4. Finish by dusting with confectioners' sugar.

Arts & Crafts Flowers

Yields about 56 cookies

These creations are reminiscent of a motif from the Arts and Crafts movement, a
period that was characterized by quality of craftsmanship and purity of design.

YOU WILL NEED

•Sugar cookie recipe (page 21) or
shortbread recipe (page 20)

•Oval cutter

•Chocolate glaze recipe (page 24)—
dark, red, yellow, and green

1. Preheat the oven to 350°F. Roll the dough to ¼ inch. Cut
the cookies with the oval cutter, and then bake for 10–12 minutes. Let the cookies cool.

2. Use a parchment paper cone to pipe the dark
chocolate outline of a flower and leaves, echoing the oval
shape of the cookie.

3. Fill in the outline with colored chocolates, reserving the
green for the leaves. Do this carefully, keeping the colored
chocolates within the piped outline. Use dark chocolate to fill
the center.

4. If necessary or desirable, trace over the initial outlines with
dark chocolate.

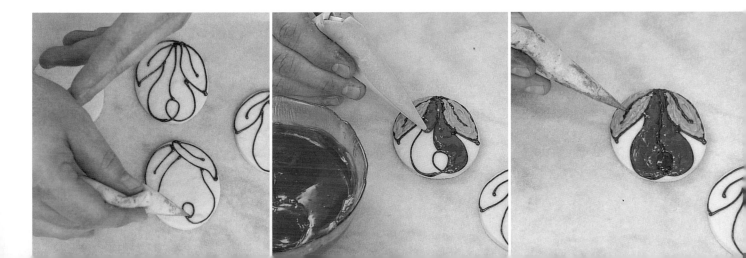

Ganache Crowns

Yields about 36 cookies

These regal confections are fit for royalty. The white chocolate exterior is ethereal; the ganache interior extraordinary.

YOU WILL NEED

- Sugar cookie recipe (page 21) or shortbread recipe (page 20)

- Round cutter

- Chocolate ganache recipe (page 24)— two times the basic recipe

- Chocolate glaze recipe (page 24)— dark, white, green, and yellow

1. Preheat the oven to 350°F. Roll the dough to ¼ inch. Cut with the round cutter and bake for 10–12 minutes. Allow the cookies to cool.

2. Prepare the chocolate ganache, and allow it to cool and set at room temperature. Using a pastry bag and large star tip, pipe rosettes of ganache on the cookies. Place the crowns in the freezer to harden the ganache.

3. Dip the crowns in the white chocolate glaze, coating each one as completely as possible; this will also seal the ganache to the cookie.

4. To complete, use a parchment paper bag to stripe each crown with colored chocolates.

Decorated Tiles

Yields about 56 cookies

These extraordinary cookies reflect the skill of a true craftsperson. Employ several techniques shown earlier to make an impressive assortment.

YOU WILL NEED

- Sugar cookie recipe (page 21) or shortbread recipe (page 20)
- Square cutter
- Chocolate glaze recipe (page 24)— dark, white, and the colors of your choice
- Toothpick
- Paintbrush
- Embellishments, such as hazelnuts and gold dragées

1. Preheat the oven to 350°F. Roll the dough to ¼ inch and cut it with a square cutter. Bake for 10–12 minutes. When the cookies are cool, dip the face of each cookie into the appropriate chocolate glaze, but read the directions completely before you begin—some designs need to set, while others must be created while the glaze is wet.

2. To create the cookie with the hazelnut centerpiece, use the same marbling technique as shown on page 93, but drag in from the outside only. Remember to work quickly, while both chocolates are still liquid, and add the hazelnut before the chocolate sets.

3. To make the blue and white cookie, let the white chocolate set and then paint on the blue chocolate as on page 51; finish the seam with a row of dots in blue chocolate, piped with a parchment paper cone. Finish with the geometric piping as shown on page 35.

4. To create the dark chocolate cookie, work while the chocolate is still liquid to make a floral motif with graceful lines of white chocolate, accented by dots representing leaves. Add other details as desired.

5. To make the white chocolate cookie with the dark chocolate embellishment, you must work quickly after you dip the cookie into the white chololate glaze. Use a parchment paper bag to create draping (gentle loops) along the edges of the cookie; see this technique below and on page 19.

6. To finish the white chocolate cookie, create the center star by adding a dot of chocolate and using a toothpick to draw lines out from the center, working quickly while the chocolate is still wet. Add the dragées before the chocolate sets.

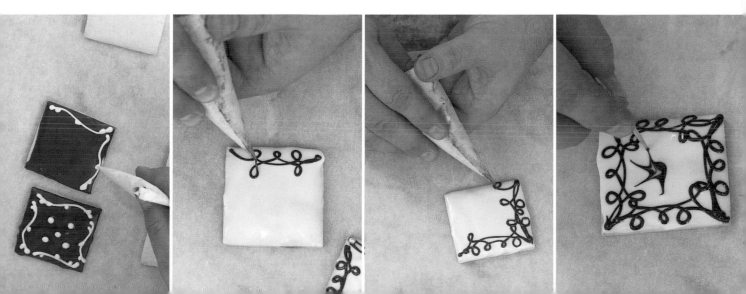

Equivalents and Metric Conversions

Weight Equivalents
Cups (c) & Ounces (oz)

1 c granulated sugar = 8 oz

1 c brown sugar, packed = 6 oz

1 c confectioners' sugar = 4½ oz

1 c all-purpose flour (unsifted) = 5 oz

1 c cake flour (unsifted) = 4½ oz

1 c chopped chocolate = 5 oz

1 c cocoa powder = 3⅔ oz

1 c finely ground hazelnuts = 4 oz

1 c slivered almonds = 4½ oz

1 c butter = 8 oz

Dry Measuring Equivalents
Teaspoons (tsp), Tablespoons (Tbsp), & Cups (c)

3 tsp = 1 Tbsp

8 tbsp = ½ c

16 tbsp = 1 c

Liquid Measuring Equivalents
Tablespoons (Tbsp) & Cups (c)

1 oz = 2 Tbsp

4 oz = ½ c

8 oz = 1 c

Approximate Weight Conversions

Ounces (oz) & Pounds (lb)	Grams (g)
¼ oz =	7 g
⅓ oz =	10 g
½ oz =	14 g
1 oz =	28 g
2 oz =	57 g
3 oz =	85 g
4 oz (¼ lb) =	113 g
8 oz (½ lb) =	226 g
16 oz (1 lb) =	454 g

Approximate Temperature Conversions

F (Fahrenheit) =	C (Celsius)
32° (water freezes) =	0°
203° (simmer) =	95°
212° (boil) =	100°
230° (blow or souffle) =	110°
300° oven, slow =	150°
350° oven, moderate =	180°
375° oven, moderately hot =	190°
400° oven, hot =	200°

Approximate Liquid Conversions

Spoons & Cups	Milliliters (mL)
1 tsp =	5 mL
2 tsp =	10 mL
3 tsp (1 Tbsp) =	15 mL
¼ c =	60 mL
⅓ c =	80 mL
1 c =	240 mL
½ c =	120 mL

Approximate Length Conversions

Inches & Feet	Centimeters (cm)
⅛ inch =	3 mm
¼ inch =	6 mm
½ inch =	1.3 cm
1 inch =	2.5 cm
4 inches =	10.2 cm
8 inches =	20.3 cm
12 inches (1 foot) =	30.5 cm
20 inches =	50.8 cm

Acknowledgments

I would like to express my thanks to Mom and Dad, for not laughing at the boy who wanted to bake. Thank you to Jeff Piccirillo, Dave Rowland, and my entire Grove Park Inn family, including my pastry team: James Hall, Lance Ethridge, Carroll Dougall, Yelka Gamboa, John Roccaforte, Rebecca Plank, Jennifer McCracken, and Lucy Smith.

Thanks to Valerie Shrader, Tom Metcalf, Sandra Stambaugh, and the entire crew at Lark Books, for being so easy to work with. Thank you to Wayne Chrebet and the New York Jets, for inspiration beyond baking.

A special expression of gratitude to my sons Daniel and Schuyler: you two are my greatest source of pride, thank you for letting me dream through you! Finally, thank you to my beautiful wife Yvonne: I love you.

Index